Negatism®

Kevin Wenig CPA

Published by www.Negatism.com

DEDICATION

To John T, Arthur H and Russell S who taught me my three most important business lessons to date.

To Ken T, who taught me everything else.

To Harrison and Lilly, to whom I give bad advice almost daily.

To The Chief – I have yet to find a business mistake he's made, despite being self-employed for decades. His contributions are the subject of another book.

To Noreen, who still comes home every night regardless of how many or how large my mistakes were that day.

TABLE OF CONTENTS

INTRODUCTION

I had just read how I should work a four-hour workweek. It was a great book, but I didn't find it practical in my particular case. Soon after, I was in Borders Books perusing the business section. I was looking for sage wisdom written by people who knew better than me how to succeed. What I soon realized was that all of these successful people wanted me to do what worked for them to be as successful as they were. Unfortunately, they have different personalities than me. They also have different financial standings, different industries, different goals, different geographical locations, different time constraints, etc. There was no way I could be like them and unfortunately, if I was not, I would not succeed. At least that's what I thought.

Then it dawned on me. What I was looking for was not advice on how others have succeeded but rather advice on what NOT to do to succeed. Things that don't work. Things I should avoid and not waste time or money doing. Things that others have tried thinking that they were good ideas but ended up being ultimately failures.

I then imagined a place where people could speak freely and give bad advice that would be universally bad for everyone, regardless of who, what or where you were.

Negatism® was born.

When reading, it's easy to notice the trends that formed in the submissions I received. There are many on how to deal with employees and there is a common theme running throughout.

Conversely, there are not many Negatisms submitted about advertising. You can draw your own conclusions, but maybe the lesson is there is no such thing as bad press?

The submissions contained in the book (and on the website) are real, submitted by real people who have been there and tried the methods themselves... all with the best of intentions. This is not meant to be a textbook, but rather a fun, almost self-deprecating guide as to what happened to other entrepreneurs. Some entries have been edited, changed or maybe we took some liberties adding some text to make it a bit more readable. Some we deleted or flat out refused to include for any number of reasons. Don't see yours? Sorry, but your advice was not as bad as I was hoping for. Stop being so negative.

EMPLOYEES

"You learn far more from negative leadership than from positive leadership. Because you learn how not to do it. And, therefore, you learn how to do it."
—*Norman Schwarzkopf*

Employee references. My biggest mistake was not talking to a prospective employee's previous employers. I should have done my homework to avoid problems later.
Gary
CEO
Technology Sales

I didn't curtail unprofessional behavior in a professional setting soon enough and was left with not only a compromised employee but they affected their coworkers as well.
Traci
Facility Manager

Giving too many "second chances" before dealing out serious punishments. In the end I had to fire them anyway. It cost me a whole lot of extra time and effort plus it hurt my relationships with the employees that were doing a great job.
Charles
Hospital Supervisor

Not firing an employee sooner.
Ed
Public Safety

Finding good employees was the biggest step for me. Knowing when you need help and when to let go along of good employees who can help you see your business in a new and sometimes better way.
Alayne
Small Business Owner

Employees have caused me the most trouble, and they were the ones I never called the references for.
Scott
Dentist

My biggest mistake was hiring a friend and thinking that she could handle my company while I was away. By doing so, my accounts had not been checked done for payment and my books were a complete wreck when I realized this later.
Lisa
Business Owner

Employees

I don't operate a business. However, the biggest mistake I've made as a supervisor is trusting people. Trust should be hard earned! I think George Washington said it best: "Be courteous to all, but intimate with few; and let those be well-tried before you give them your confidence."
Anonymous
Education Director

I wouldn't have the "hey were all friends" type of attitude again. I'm the boss, do as I say. I'd be open to your suggestions, but do as I ask.
NH
Entrepreneur
Multiple Small Businesses

Delegate. Delegate. Delegate.
KB
Owner
Professional Services

Make sure they're fully and properly trained before leaving them on their own.
Your crew must work for a boss.
Margaret
Realtor
Real Estate

I kept trying to work with subordinates who did not like working with me even though they had allies in senior management.
Anonymous
Department Head
Publishing

I gave my friend a job and she blew it.
Anonymous
Manager
Fast Food Restaurant

Don't trust the wrong people. Understanding people are out for themselves especially if they have nothing invested in your relationship other than your money.
RB
Entrepreneur
Corporate Consulting

If an employee is flagging and putting off getting their work done, reverse the attitude or let them go. We held on to some employees too long, and when we needed them the most, they abandoned us, taking some of our customers with them. They copied our software and walked it out the door, and also badmouthed us, trying to lure other customers away. It was a blatant betrayal of trust, and completely unethical behavior. What was especially bad was that one of the partners thought that the betrayer was a close personal friend. The psychological damage for that individual lasted for years. They became largely diminished in their desire to even come to work for at least two years. We had to work very hard to rebuild what we lost, recover, and grow.

TS
Partner
Financial Services

My biggest mistake was to not follow the rules and keep confidentiality. I work in mental health and did not listen to the rules concerning patient privacy and was embarrassed.

Anonymous
Certified Peer Support Specialist
Healthcare

Do not trust outside agents. I only trust employees within my company. I would not call agents to assist in business in the future, I will promote from within and delegate.

LW
CFO
Healthcare Supplies

I hired the wrong people because I didn't vet them properly and I there was no probationary period.
DC
Medical Doctor
Group Practice

I was too lenient on the employees and tried to be a friend. I couldn't find balance. If I could have a do over, I would reach out to them in a more professional way to show them respect but not allow me to come across as a pushover.
JG
Owner
Home Décor

I did not plan enough to avoid certain problems concerning ensuring my payroll was sufficiently funded at all times.
EA
Marketing

I hired a friend. Never again.
EV
CEO
Food Service

I hired inept employees. If I would have emailed references or asked more questions I could have avoided this.
TT
Manager
Hospitality

Don't under-value your staff. Get the right group of people who are self-motivated to get the job done, even if you have to pay them more, it just works best.

Don't think you are befriending your employees. They do not think of you as a friend and are there for one reason – to earn a paycheck. When they laugh at your jokes, it's because they are plotting their next raise.

Fire a disgruntled employee. Today. They poison the well and will never be happy, no matter what you do for them.

Don't stress at work. Keep calm at all times. If you need a few minutes, walk away and catch your breath.
KJ
Restaurateur
Multiple Restaurants

Biggest mistake is trusting your employees to look out for your best interests, only you can do that. I've been self-employed full-time since 1980, and the overriding principle of each and every one was to make more and more money, and business be damned.
Anonymous
Engineer/ Attorney

Never hire someone who is not at least as smart as you.
Bill
Owner
Retail

Don't have too many junior employees or trainees at one time.
FR
Medical Doctor
Private Practice

I thought employee management would be easy – it's not. Take extra HR classes and be prepared for tons of employee drama.
Anonymous

Don't hire part-time employees thinking you'll save money over a full-time employee. Part timers have somewhere else to be and are less productive than the person trying to impress you because this is their career.
Stella
Owner
Small Manufacturing Business

I kept employees too long after the downturn. Should have laid people off early 2009 and did not do so until 15 months later.
ZF
Owner
Large Retail Store

I would have a "no jerks" rule and use the probationary period to fire jerks, no matter how talented and skillful they may be.
Larry
CEO
Tech Start-Up

Employees

First we would not hire friends and family. Second, we would be more demanding of employees and not treat them as friends. We would have been more productive if we were somewhat sterner.

Anonymous
Proprietor
Retail Bakery

It does not matter how much you pay them, give them mentorship, opportunities etc. Life changes and so do people. Plan for their exit and always have a 2nd in place who is capable.

TJ
Entrepreneur

Negatism®

Maintain a friendly work atmosphere, but keep a certain amount of distance between you and your employees. Employees, and especially family, can take advantage of friendships.
Anonymous
Vice president
Environmental Consulting Firm

I hired a couple friends, and it made it difficult to keep that line defined between boss and friend. It caused problems and misunderstandings. Both found other jobs, but the friendship was never the same. Other staff also felt like they were being treated differently even though they were not. But the perception was there just because we were friends. If I did hire friends again, I would have to make clearly defined rules for us and make sure they were respected by all.
PC
Education Director

Starting a company with a white collar unionized workforce and I spent most of my time babysitting instead of leading. It was Impossible to get rid of underperforming people.
TT
CEO
Credit Union

Paid employees from a line of credit when I should have let them go. I would never allow myself to be abused by my employee, no matter how much I needed them.
AY
Co-owner
Pest Control

I once had an employee who had serious issues with drugs and other personal problems, and I didn't realize how bad it was until she was taking advantage of me so much that I was covering her shifts all the time and it was making me look bad to my customers. Fired her eventually, but it took a while to recover from it.
Anonymous
Manager
Septic Company

Don't make friends with your employees.
KMD
Owner
Daycare

Employees have a different motivation than you do. Don't trust they will act in your best interest.
SM

Don't ever let your employees know how much you earn. They'll look at you differently.
RB
Engineer
Digital Asset Production

If you have the opportunity to eavesdrop on your employees, DON'T! You won't like what they say and you'll never forget what you heard.
TF
Accountant

Don't ever hire a family member. Ever. Dumbest thing I ever did. She was terrible and likely thinks the same of me. Now, it's awkward every time we see each other. She is also talking about me to my other relatives. I wish I never tried to be the nice guy and help my cousin out. Be sure to check on employees work, even if they assure you that they've done it. Don't assume doing business with friends doesn't require due diligence.
TRM
CEO
Healthcare

Don't get involved with union labor.
Anonymous

I tried outsourcing some repetitive tasks to a company in India thinking I would save money. This was a huge mistake. It took time from me and my staff to train people who worked different times than we did. Although English speaking and certainly willing to help, they often understood the directions we gave them differently than what we intended. Everything took so long and e-mails took a day to send and a day to answer. The investment was far too great to make it worthwhile for us.
RJ
Bookkeeping

I made the dumbest mistake of all. I confided in an employee I thought of as a friend and spoke negatively about another one of my employees. Of course, she told him what I said.

TF

Livery Service

Biggest lesson I've learned is that while it can take years to build a good reputation and establish trust with your customers, it can all be undone very quickly. As our business grew and we started hiring more employees, we became aware that you are only as good as the tech you send out in the field. A few with substandard work ethics can drag down your good name in a hurry. So it's vital to make employees accountable for the work they do and reward those who go above and beyond for the customer. And have an additional layer of oversight to assure quality control.

MS

Manager

HVAC

CLITENTS

"A deadline is negative inspiration. Still, it's better than no inspiration at all."
—*Rita Mae Brown*

Not being pro-active enough
Basil
Owner
Financial Planning

Do not alienate your customers. Always make them feel welcome and appreciated. The more they like the way they feel in your store, the more time they will spend there, and the more money the will spend.
Anonymous
Manager
Retail

The biggest mistake I've made was underpricing myself, and accepting commissions that were a waste of time. Be picky. It saves time in the long run.
Anonymous
Owner
Commissioned Original Fine Art

I underestimated my market. I was the only one in the area and assumed people would come to me because of it.
SG
Owner
Consulting

If you're selling something do not push too much information but ask questions and know what you're selling. Not having product knowledge only looses sales and makes employees look like a liability rather than an asset.
Anonymous
Wholesale Auto Parts

Never, ever blame the customer. Wish I'd learned that sooner.
Anonymous
PC Sales and Service

My biggest mistake has been not being as client friendly as I could have been. It has cost me work and referrals.
DES
Owner
Interior Design

Selling products that I had to order from a wholesaler. No matter what their size they were unreliable.
JSF
Owner
IT Consulting

Don't play to people's weaknesses. Thinking that I could learn at least one thing from everyone.
TR
Sales director
Catering & Food Service

I'm an attorney and when I started, I would take any case I could get, even if it wasn't in my area of expertise. I wish I had known from the beginning that this was a terrible idea. It is always better to refer clients to those who can assist them   best.
RAC
Partner
Legal Firm

Not asking for the sale.
Anonymous
Realtor

The biggest mistake I ever made was not listening to my intuition and sticking with a bad client when every thing told me to walk away.
KLB
Co-owner
Real Estate Staging

Not following up with a client after a transaction and then I became impatient when the client asked questions after the transaction was completed.
JP
Realtor
Commercial Real Estate

Not stand up for myself and ask for higher fees instead of settling. I was late in realizing that if I didn't express confidence in myself and value my work then how could expect others to respect me.
RB
Administrator
Healthcare

It is the golden rule of business, whether it be gods or services, we must learn that the customer is always right. Do not argue with customers; try to please them.
DW
Coach

Conquering cold calling. Wouldn't start a new business.
If a customer is really wrong, don't give in to them.
I would never have signed a Non-Compete Agreement with a company I had no reason to trust in order to keep the client.
RA
Co-owner
Small Business

Working closely with and supporting the project manager of a client who was "on the outs." I didn't recognize that and so I lost the client when he lost his job.
Anonymous

Try to satisfy every potential customer no matter what they asked for.
NS
System Engineer
Satellite Communications

Don't set up a new business based on the wants of a current client and expect them to follow you from the old company to my new company automatically, even if they indicated they would. Sometimes people change their minds and it is best to not count on things before they happen.
CA
Agent
Industrial Inspection

Don't let the customers get to you, if you work in retail or the service industry. Just remember that they'll be gone in a few minutes and without them you may not have a job.
Anonymous

Once you screw up a client, drop them. They will always remember that time when things went awry and will remind you of it as soon as things seem off again.
Barb
Owner
Corporate Catering

Your customers don't like you as much as you think they do. Think of who you would stay in touch with if you sold the business. None of them.
Anonymous
Serial Restaurateur

Be kind to customers always.
Anonymous

Too trusting and not looking out after myself enough. Not making my clients (patients) always pay their fair share.
LKR
PhD.

I failed to clarify the value proposition before soliciting clients hence I had a sloppy, uninspiring pitch, which didn't get prospects to convert. Once I learned to put myself in my clients' shoes and identify what problem was going to be solved for them by my service, it was much easier to make the sale.
DF
CEO
IT Consulting

Telling a client I would do something and taking too long to get it done. It hurt their trust in me and tarnished my reputation
KB
Financial Advisor

Never tell a dirty joke to a client.
CH
Medical Technologies

Never assume you know how the client will respond & always notify them before changing something on their listing to get it approved.
GV
Broker
Real Estate

It doesn't matter if you're right. Don't lose a customer over it.
RL
Restaurateur

Don't ever sound unsure of yourself when giving a client professional advice. No one wants to trust someone who doesn't trust themselves. Have doubts? Give a range of possibilities if you can't nail it down exactly. Or, consider resigning from the client if you can't handle it.
JT
Supply Chain Coordinator

Don't give too many things away trying to be nice, that was my biggest mistake. Charge for anything not on contract.
TAH
General Contractor

Do not rely on one or two customers. Easy to say, I know. But if that's your business model, you will fail.
Steve
Owner
Small Business

If you run your business and manage cash flow with the assumption your clients will pay on time, you are heading for disaster.
Anonymous

Don't do extras without a contract.
TB
Freelancer
Tech Industries

Not keeping an eye on my customers activity and don't start a job without a deposit.
AZ
Co-owner
Wildlife Management

Don't do anything without a paper trail (contracts, invoices, receipts), whether for legal or tax purposes.
Anonymous
Music Education Studio

Clients

I stayed with a client who paid me less than I'm worth. I wish someone warned me not to get too comfortable with the routine. I've repeatedly sold myself short. I will regret my cowardice for the rest of my life.
Anonymous
Corporate Recruiter
Bookseller

Don't pitch a client who needs very specific skills that you do not have and try to "pad" your experience hoping you can somehow figure it out later. Don't promise what you can't provide, be on time, price, or quality.
Anonymous
Contractor

FEES

"Chase the vision, not the money. The money will end up following you."
—*Tony Hseih, Zappos CEO*

Not charging enough for my services.
CVJ
Freelancer

Failing to properly collect the money we were owed.
Anonymous
Tech Company

Don't work on speculation unless you're prepared to take a loss.
Anonymous
Design

I under estimating what people would pay for my service.
Contracts are not worth the paper written on unless you have a lot of money to sue
Don't sacrifice your profit margin to help the customer. It is rarely appreciated.
WJ
Owner

Transportation/ Trucking
I wished I would have charged what I was worth rather than underpricing myself.
ZP
Videographer

Charge more for your services. People will buy based upon a correlation of high prices equal quality.
Anonymous
Owner
Limousine Service

Don't undercut your price. You work harder, have less money and the client thinks you are only worth that much. If you are not confident in yourself enough to raise your fees, then you should not be in business. I'm a professional commissioned portrait artist; the best advice I could give to those looking to enter this field is not to underprice your work. Do your research, and ask for advice.
JNX
Artist

I gave away my services for free, on more than one occasion and not for some charitable organization either.
BP
Spanish Interpreter

I underpriced my services at the very beginning. It was extremely difficult to get clients to the right price point from there.
Anonymous
Accountant

Don't set your prices too low to attract customers. Those aren't the customers you want, anyway.
Don't set prices based on what competition is charging, but determine all of your costs and set your prices accordingly.
AJM
Co-owner
Towing and Auto Repair

STRUCTURE

"Negative attitude is nine times more powerful
than positive attitude."
—*Bikram Choudhury*

I would have not taken on such a broad category of services, but focused on one or two, and waited for those to bring fruit, rather than being so scattershot hoping something would stick. I would also structure things so I would not have to do so much myself.
TJ
Lawyer
Private Practice

I also think one can fall into a work culture where being busy, being swamped etc. feels competitive, like a measure of your worth. I now realize that this sort of environment doesn't have to be the norm. An efficient person who can delegate is just as valuable, likely more so, than the person who's trying to take everything on themselves.
JTM
Practice Manager
Veterinary Hospital

Doing it without having thought out a plan B. For everything. Down to the printers to print invoices. Everything in duplicate. Plan for the worst and hope for the best. You must Be Proactive.
Anonymous
Franchise Owner
Retail Chain

Trusting someone without a clearly designed contract of responsibilities and a clear direct job outline.
Anonymous
Personal Manager
Entertainment

Don't quit selling while your managing your pipeline of business. Find someone who isn't as busy as you and have them help manage your pipeline so you can keep selling.
BV
Vice President
Financial Institution

The biggest mistake I made in business was trusting that someone who was supposed to be a family friend would be honest and reliable after opening businesses in a joint building with him. He refused to sign any kind of agreement and almost immediately started going back on all of the verbal agreements we had made. Since there was nothing to prove that he had made those agreements in the first place I had no recourse and things ended badly.
ALT
Owner
Bakery

Sending out a report immediately after I've finished it, rather than waiting until I've had a chance to put it down, then open it up again and go through it with fresh eyes. I nearly always catch mistakes.
Anonymous
Director
Marketing Research

Cover all our bases legally and no matter how kind someone seems, always assume they are looking for a way to drag you into a lawsuit.
Anonymous
Owner/Operator
Woodworking

I wish I closed the business when my partner retired. He left because he saw the writing on the wall with the flood of cheap imported goods flooding the market.
WM
President
Manufacturing

Don't let your first idea be your best idea. The first one (or even the first several) will fail.
KJW
Serial Entrepreneur

Bought products to resell but I couldn't sell any of them. I put a lot of money into inventory.
Anonymous
Owner
Online Retail

Not getting an MBA
Anonymous
Dentist
Clinical Practice

Not carefully analyzing my first work product before starting my second and third.
QM
Engineer
R&D

Don't delay in creating a website. It's the first place people look.
Anonymous

I opened a shared office with someone I barely knew on the advice of other people I barely knew.
Mike
Owner
Law Firm

Picking the wrong partners is a big one for me. I tried to start several projects with partners from scratch and each time I found that we were not compatible with each other.
Anonymous

Some people do great things all by themselves. Not me. I've come to accept that I need a team – or at least a teammate.
GJL
CEO
Technology

Do not take a partner. Money will separate you; there will be hard feelings and at the most a lawsuit. Or, as In my case, criminal prosecution of my partner.
Anonymous
Owner/ Partner
Bar

Don't stretch yourself too thin. Know when to ask for help.
KH
Artist and Designer

I did not ask enough questions before handing over money to buy into the franchise.
LD
Owner
Restaurant Franchise

Working from home means you're always working and you never turn off.
Anonymous

I would not do an ESOP – there are simpler and more effective ways to share ownership with employees.
Terry

My biggest mistake is I let my ego get in the way of the most important aspect of a business, teamwork.
Anonymous
Partner
Law Firm

Consider your business as a glass half empty situation. By focusing on what could go wrong, and fixing it and planning for it, you will improve your outcomes dramatically, by being ready for objections and other sure to occur challenges.
Jordan
CPA
Financial Group

I wish I learned to delegate better rather than feeling like I need to do everything myself.
JK
Office Manager
Contractor

Instead take the $25,000 to $40,000 franchise fee and spending a few thousands on classes – then go do it yourself. You're not only saving the franchise fee, you will not be paying royalties of 19% percent like I was for no local or national marketing. Instead, use the cash saving from the franchise as operating cash, and use the franchise royalties as marketing money.
PKR
Restaurateur

I wish someone had told me about the "unknowns" of owning a company. It's not as easy as people think. You can't just start a company and be selling on day one.
JB
President
Fire Safety Sales and Service

Starting a small business requires more than word of mouth advertising and a higher level of knowledge regarding taxes.
Anonymous

Not working it hard enough.
RM
Owner
Boutique

I would have not waited so long to go independent
KLJ
President
Finance

Not getting things in writing. Never make agreements over the phone without getting it in writing. Even an email or text message, anything that you can see or more importantly, that a judge could see.
TMK
CEO
Government Contractor

We had all heard the same explanation of the plan and had all been trained. To me, the task straightforward, I assumed it was the same for everyone and we ended up having to redo half the work. Never assume everyone's "got it" and is on the same page, verbally check.
JW
Management
Warehouse

Being in business was not for me, so I retired.
Anonymous
Mary Kay Consultant

Hiring family. Don't. Just don't.
RR
CEO
Food Service

I learned how to run a business from my shittiest bosses. It's simple, just don't be like them.
BL
CEO
Advertising

Structure

Don't buy someone else's business. Start your own.
MH
Owner
Automotive Repair

I mistakenly decided to sell inexpensive items (books) rather than specialize on more expensive books.
RHS
President
Bookseller

Do not go into business with someone without a written contract.
PG
Owner
Publishing Small Press

Don't be easily swayed by the influence of others who may not have your best interest in mind, trust your intuition.
CS
Owner
Retail

Start a business without contacting an accountant and a lawyer.
Sandy
Owner
Specialty Bakery

Keep up on changes in technology, don't get left behind.
Anonymous
IT Consultant

Taking the present/current situation for granted, assuming that it will always be that way; the recession changed everything and there will be more.
PM
President
Management Consulting

I tried to do too many things when starting up a new venture; that is, including too many extra features and services instead of focusing on the main thing. Now customers expect all of these perks that aren't worth my time to engage in.
GF
Creative Director
Publishing

Never share material or ideas with anyone if they are not copyright protected.
CW
Owner
Retail

Don't give up. You'll likely fail at first but so did most successful companies. Just keep visualizing your goal. Don't try to be and do everything in the business. Do what you do best, and outsource, or hand off the rest.
PMW

FINANCIAL

"You can't live a positive life with a negative mind and if you have a positive outcome, you have positive income and just to have more positivity and just to kind of laugh it off."
—*Miley Cyrus*

Taxes. Pay them first, no matter what. The government always wins.
Anonymous
Administrator
Family Business

I would not let financial success handcuff me to a business that I was no longer passionate about. I'd sell it and move on quicker, I can use the skills I have learned to do something I AM passionate about!
RB
Financial Consultant

The biggest mistake I made in business was the need to start with enough capital. My first business grew way too fast, choking out my capital requirements and forcing me to slow down my growth until I could finance steady growth. I would never start a business without more than enough capital again.
RH
President
Pest Control

Not reinvesting profit.
DN

Don't invest in a restaurant. Their rate of failure is so high and they require so much work that only an owner would kill themselves to make their restaurant a success and even then they have to be very passionate.
DS
Owner
Wholesaler

I wish I had started with more working capital so I could get through the lean times easier; especially for equipment maintenance. I wouldn't buy used equipment in such bad shape requiring so much time and money again. What I thought was a bargain ended up costing me more than newer equipment would have in the first place.
GC
Restaurateur

Financial

If I could do it over, I would take my college education more seriously. I would participate in extra projects and internships. At my job, I would take more risks, focus on goals, take steps to advance and make my goals known to employers. I'd learn basic accounting practices and keep up with technology.
SH
President
Title Company

I wish someone had told me not to wait till I have enough capital to start my own business; that with the small capital I had, I could start something small and grow from there. I wish they had told me that business is perseverance, trust, patience and acting "stingy." This way I would have made it big while I was still young and energetic. But hey, it is never too late. I am using what I learned now to make a GREAT ENDING!!!
MCJ
Owner
Event Planning

Make sure you have emergency cash on hand, because you never know when you will need it.
Anonymous
Owner
Custodial Services

Do NOT purchase more inventory than you know you can sell!
DM
CEO
Manufacturing

My biggest mistake was not finding a credible and reliable accountant early on. I learned that owning a business does not mean that you get a ton of money back by writing things off. If given the opportunity, I truly would not have gone into business for myself at all.
HR
Owner
Day Care

Be sure you are going to have the income projected before purchasing the business. IE: We could see adequate income from previous years, but the year we purchased, salmon fishing, which was the big money maker for us, was banned... making purchasing of the business a hardship and causing concern about this happening in the future and future viability of it. It is hard to get recreational fishermen to book your Salmon-fishing charter business when they can't catch any Salmon.
MS
Owner/ Partner
Salmon Fishing Expeditions

The biggest mistake I made in business was throwing away my receipts. A lot of my supplies could have been written off had I kept them. When I did my taxes, the agent helping informed me of the benefits of keeping receipts.
GG
Owner
Retail

The biggest mistake was not putting money (even a little) away for rainy days. We have been in business for 38 years and have always spent as it came in.
Anonymous

We did not plan for retirement/investments. That's by far our biggest mistake.
Margie
Owner
Family Business

Barter = Bad. Both parties always feel like they got the short end of the stick.
Anonymous

A huge mistake I made was not having enough in capital reserves for the lean months/years.
Anonymous
Owner
Cafe

I would maintain personal control and accounting of corporate cash on a daily basis.
LRD
Founder/ CEO
Technology Consultant

I wish someone told me to get a line of credit when I DIDN'T need it. Banks won't give you one when you do need it.
Anonymous

My biggest mistake was spending the money when I earned it. If I could do it all over again, I would keep three months of overhead in the bank. Trust me you'll need it eventually.
Mike
Restaurateur
Multiple Locations

Don't Sign a 5-year lease with a large rent based on a budget. Budgets don't always work out, especially when you are making them with no experience in the business.
D
Owner/ Designer
Boutique

Don't pay professionals a salary and hope they perform. Pay them a percentage of what they bill.
NR
Owning Partner
Law Firm

Don't undercapitalize!
Anonymous

Never trust a stockbroker.
DC
Doctor
Private Practice

Borrow as a last resort; you never can have enough cash on hand.
Anonymous
Owner
Restaurant

Not cost accounting enough, and missing out on the profits.
JC
CEO
Retail Bakery

Don't control the expenses. Save that for those who are good at it.
BMR
Manager
Telecommunications

You can't work solely for money, you must work for happiness too.
K
Consultant
Financial

Don't Invest Foolishly. Money is hard to come by. Treat it with respect.
Anonymous

Don't trust anyone else with the financials; make sure you know what is happening with your money at all times.
RK
Owner
Retail

Don't overextend. That's it.
Anonymous

Don't begin a project with inadequate financing. Wait until you know you have enough funding to pull off the project in the event of all possible developments.
BE
Editorial Director
Publishing

Don't start a business that is not VERY properly defined in terms of needs. Don't start a business without the expectation that the first years are going to be difficult. Check your level of commitment and the commitment of your FAMILY. Don't start a business without proper financial backing or knowing where you will find additional financial support to sustain your business.

RN
Executive Director
Consulting Firm

Get the line of credit when business is doing well and you don't need it. The banks won't give you credit when you actually need. Qualify, secure the credit, and then don't use it until you need it.

TH
Professional Athlete

I shouldn't have assumed I'd get funding right away (or at all). Especially starting an NFP, investors don't invest in models that don't turn profits; so finding investors for NFPs is impossible.

KF
President and CEO
Not for Profit Organization

Don't start with loans, secure start up funds that don't accrue interest and won't be demanding repayment in a month or so.

AD
CEO
Business Consulting

Be prepared to lose money. If you assume you will make money out of the gate, you're a fool.
AS
Owner
Financial/ Tax Specialist

Don't forget to pay your taxes!
Anonymous

ADVERTISING

"Marketing takes a day to learn. Unfortunately, it takes a lifetime to master."
—*Phil Kolter*

I created my own advertising and would recommend speaking with an advertising/marketing specialist.
MA
Owner
Spa/ Salon

I assumed that a web page would bring business. It doesn't. You need to advertise wisely.
DMR
Owner
Personal Services

Not getting my info out there resulted in less business. I should have done more networking.
MS
Owner
Childcare/ Early Education

I would invest more time into marketing myself. I was too focused on the fire at hand to advertise.
MB
Therapist
Healthcare

Not enough marketing lead to limited new business signups and repeat customers.
EGV
Owner
Financial Planning

Stay focused and don't give up when the phone isn't ringing. Plan on marketing to newer clients and stay focused on delivering quality results. Don't be discouraged with a complaint or a downturn in business, try to learn from it and move on.
SR
Owner
Real Estate Inspection

I under estimated the cost of self-promoting a business and the time requirement devoted to marketing and keeping up with social media. Now, I know that when people say they work in social media management, that it is easily a full-time job.
JTD
Co-founder
Travel Agency

Not paying my taxes correctly, and a not advertising.
AFA
CEO
Healthcare

Don't rely on third parties to generate business.
RTT
Owner
Law Practice

Google ads, Facebook promos, Twitter ads... Just pay what they are asking. It's worth it. What was I thinking? I shouldn't have assumed word of mouth was enough advertising, I needed to be on as many screens as I could.
KF
President and CEO
Not for Profit Organization

I thought I knew what social media was, how it worked and how to do it effectively. I didn't see the value in hiring someone when I thought 'how hard can it be' and could do it myself. If I could do it over again, hiring a pro would be a bigger priority.
RTJ
Founder & CEO
Corporate Consulting

Don't skimp on advertising. Trying to get the word out in the cheapest ways possible rarely gives very good returns.
JB
Owner/ Operator
Restaurant

INFRASTRUCTURE

"The essence of strategy is choosing what
not to do."
—*Michael Porter, Bishop William Lawrence University
Professor at Harvard Business School*

When it comes to bringing on investors, do homework. Just because someone has money that you want doesn't mean they have morals or histories that you want to be associated with.
Anonymous
Administrator
Healthcare

My biggest mistake was that I didn't invest in my own business in order for it to grow.
Anonymous
Owner
Professional Services

My lack of oversight and not tracking supplies and expenses against a budget. Ignoring a small detail can snowball into a nightmare.
Anonymous
CEO and President
Industrial Supplies

Not understanding the politics of a situation with a regulatory agency.
Anonymous
Nonprofit/ Healthcare

Not applying proper training to other management team members. This only makes everyone's jobs harder and I now train everyone to know the next position to move in to. I needed to implement better time management.
EB
Executive Director
Not for Profit Organization

Not developing a thoroughly crafted and vetted business plan and marketing plan.
RS
CEO
Marketing

Learn accounting. Yeah, it sucks, but understanding what you're looking at everyday, and how it effects you and your business is worth it.
WW
Owner
Retail

Lack of focus. Not so much in productivity, but in areas of service. When you try to do too much, you spread yourself too thin and the quality of your work suffers.
Anonymous
Creative Director
Design and Presentation

Not setting boundaries.
BJ
Manager
Corporate Accounts

Not seeking out more companies that are on the verge of going public with high profile products.
Anonymous
Inventor/ Entrepreneur

Never put a physical address on business cards. I've wasted lots of money having to reprint cards. Phone numbers are perfect because once you make contact you can tell your customer your location.
TG
Owner
Massage/ Physical Therapy

I did not understand that L & I was not filed by ADP and it cost me thousands and liens on my house.
Anonymous
Owner
Landscaping

My biggest mistake was allowing myself to be taken advantage of and abused by my employees. I wish I'd quit sooner.
AZ
Owner
Restaurant

Giving up.
Anonymous

Occasionally it's better to give up. So don't keep fighting against all odds, know when to cut your losses and walk away.
Anonymous

Failing to follow through when I said I would do something, I damaged important relationships.

Don't make a financial decision when upset. I once took a loan over my own "jealousy" of someone else.

Anonymous

CEO

Financial Advisor

I am the owner of a small vintage boutique. I have had this business for eight years, but had two similar businesses prior to it that were unsuccessful. The problem with both was they were located in places not well suited to the products I was offering.

GY

Owner

Retail/ Fashion

I wish someone had told me not to have ordered so much product with expiration dates of less than 3 years when I was starting my business. I am an Independent Beauty Consultant and most of the products I sell have a 3-year shelf life as long as they haven't been opened. Some of them have less than that due to ingredients that make them have to be used by a certain date. Not having been told this at first, I learned the hard way when I embarrassingly sold out of date product to a client. I was able to correct it as I had product in stock that was still in date and good for a long period of time. I however had several products on hand I had to write off. Being a new business made this a costly mistake. We don't have to carry product but I feel that it gets more sales to have the product on hand. I now know what to order for a longer shelf life and what to keep minimum amounts of as its shelf life is shorter.

CV
Owner
Beauty Consulting

Chose the wrong person to design my website. She lied about her skills, charged me $3000 and I had to trash the entire site and start over.

CK
Owner
Digital Retail

I would have organized my administration better.

CBK
Owner
Dog Training

I ordered the wrong supplies because I was in a hurry and rushed, to make it worse, I had to borrow supplies from a nearby gym.
RC
Manager
Fitness Industry

Not spending enough resources on new business development.
DDC
Owner
Entrepreneur

Not firing my partner when I knew it would be best for the business, in order to be fair to him. I should have let him go and continued on with the company I built.
Phil
CEO
Corporate Logistics

Don't forget to take care of yourself. Owning a business is a lot of work—probably more than you thought, particularly when first starting out.
Anonymous

I over-reached & exceeded capacity. I should have ben happy with what I could comfortably perform, but I making too many demands on myself only compromised the quality of my work.
DO
President
International Consulting

Be very clear in certifications needed to operate, not filing the correct paperwork and jumping through the right hoops can delay opening or worse, interrupt normal business operations.
PM
Independent
Engineering Consultant

Hard work does not always lead to success.
RK
Independent
Consulting

When you start a business, don't let other people's negative reactions effect you. Only talk about business with people who are helpful and supportive.
MH
Owner
Photography

Don't trust people you don't know or haven't done business with for a significant amount of time. Verify everything. Ask questions. Don't be shy or self-conscious over digging deeper. Don't assume you know everything. Sometimes the best information comes from entry-level people. Don't expand your business until you have the people and infrastructure to do so.
JT
CEO
Hospitality

Infrastructure

Don't assume your idea is better than others. Assume it is competitive. Don't count on a name. Don't assume people will find you. Don't assume that you will be profitable right away, so don't under-capitalize. Don't assume anything will be easy.

BP
Owner
Internet Sales

Not pushing hard enough when I thought I was right. My company had a chance to buy Oakley sunglasses in 1992 for $40M. Three years ago it was sold for $1B.
Anonymous

Don't procrastinate on doing anything that needs to be done for your business; whether it seems like it's a quick easy task or not. And don't rely on other people to help you. Always prepare to have to do it alone and if help does show up, then awesome but if not, then it won't completely screw you.

SM
Owner
Retail Jewelry

I started raising goats without developing a plan; as usual, I wanted to learn on the job. There were benefits to that but it cost me more money than it should have and now I'm playing catch-up.

AM
Partner
Farming

I followed the crowd rather than looking at the opportunities I had to create something I knew was good, but had not been done by someone else yet.
LD
Independent
Restaurant Consultant

I wish someone told me not to take a home equity line of credit to start my business. Years later, I am still feeling the effects.
NMM
Owner
Landscape Architecture

Don't undervalue your contributions.
Don't assume that everyone has your best interest in mind. Vendors will overstock your inventory at every opportunity. Don't assume that your department managers hold your business as their highest priority like you do.
RTP
Director
Aerospace

In medical school there was NO training in how to start or run a business. If you want to go into private practice someday, you will be clueless.
SWB
Doctor
Private Practice

Don't bite off more than you can chew. Be sure to try to maintain balance, not only for your mental health, but for your physical health too.
RA
Owner
Construction

When you have a really great idea, don't share it with anyone thinking they will help you. I once contacted a nationally recognized magazine that catered to self-employed people to see if they would publish a list of "what went wrong" from real business owners. They thought it would be best never to contact me again and just run with the idea themselves.
KR
Owner
Financial Firm

I wished I understood the previous owner's impact on his clients. I should have leveraged him differently rather than assuming he was old, out of date and I knew better. I lost many of his clients after the acquisition because I tried to force my "better, more up to date methods" on his long-time clients. Fail.
CPA
Owner
Retail/ Services

Don't allow business contacts to fade away even though your company has move on to another supplier or vendor. Keeping your options open for supply management is crucial during shortages or backorders.
EK
Logistics Manager
Medical Supplies

Don't open a business as a sole proprietor in my area! I should not have spent my savings to do so. I should have taken a loan at the get-go. I didn't consult with anyone or created a solid business plan.
Anonymous
CEO
Healthcare

I wish someone had told me not to cater to weakness within an organization.
DS
Administrator
Education

Not double-checking equipment maintenance.
Anonymous

I would not take any statements about facts, unless I am in the company of a court officer or court official.
VW
Advocate
Legal

"When there's so many haters and negative things,
I really don't care."
—*Kim Kardashian*

Don't have a water cooler, however, you don't need one for employees to gossip. My biggest mistake was calling an employee out (privately) for gossiping about an HR matter I inadvertently overheard, then having her run around checking with everybody about whether they'd heard it too and starting almost a mutiny as she falsely garnered support. This issue should've been sent straight to HR.
E
Facility Director
Medical R&D

Being "too nice" and not trusting my instincts. Opened business in a small town where there was literally not enough people to provide the customer base I needed.
Anonymous
Owner
Yoga and Fitness Studio

Talk to people like they are people. Like they have brains and can understand what you say. Like they have hearts that care for things like you do. Like they have a soul. Be patient. Be respectful. Be honest.
Anonymous

While in the bathroom stall with a co-worker in the next one, we began to talk about another employee and of course, she was in the bathroom. In the end and we didn't notice until she said something to us out loud. Boy, were we embarrassed. Never talk about someone even if you are sure they are not near. It's just bad form.
Anonymous
Manager
Food and Beverage

Two things: Never do business with family (or friends).
Never make business deals in a bar.
IJH
Owner
General Contractor

I didn't report unethical behavior because I didn't think anything would be done about it.
CC

Playing into gossip. There is a lot of gossip around our office, and it has the potential to be very damaging when you work in government.
Anonymous

Did not speak up and succumbed to Group Think. Always think for yourself.
DRL
Retired VP
Higher Education

Sometimes the grind pays off. Even if you aren't moving up immediately, if the company has room for growth, the grind can pay off.
JMM
Developer/ Owner
Software Company

Do not compromise your own morals to appease your superiors. I lied to a customer as directed by my employer and never got over it. Ended up quitting the job soon after anyways and I wish I did it before that.
DKA

Failure to bloom wherever I was planted.
TR
Owner
Catering

Stayed in a job for at least 2 years & was polite when upper management was being ageist and sexist. I was told to deal with it if I wanted to be promoted. The promotion never happened.
K
Administrator
Professional Services

Make friends with your peers - don't just focus on buttering up the boss - your peers are more likely to ultimately be your friends and have your back. They can help you out and keep you from looking stupid.
DMH
Partner
Law Firm

Opening my mouth when I should have just kept quiet.
GM

Listening to people who don't actually own a business is a waste of time.
BB
Owner
Sales

Do not go behind anyone's back, it always backfires.
Jay
Kitchen Manager
Hotel

Don't be everyone's friend.
Anonymous
Doctor
Group Practice

NEVER do business in bars!
Anonymous

Lying to any customers, vendors or employees.
DB
Owner
Industrial Electric

Don't offer advice without being sure it is wanted.
BJ

Trusted people with good intentions to be ethical in their dealings... they were not.
Anonymous

Never give a lot of details about family, friendships. Be very neutral as it can be used against you in certain scenarios, especially on social media.
SO
Partner
Dance Studio

Don't assume people know what you do!
Anonymous

Don't answer questions specific to your expertise from people who don't pay you for the answers you provide. Information is a commodity,
MOR
CEO
Educational Services

Don't assume a person cc'd on an email agrees with anything that was written. Resorting to personal attacks against the cc'd individual is classless and can only serve a negative purpose.
Lauren
Administrator
Large Tech Firm

Loyalty is not valued, trust no one.
PM
Social Media Manager
Start-up Nonprofit

Avoid gossip and giving medical device.
Sam
Owner
Yoga Studio

To be too trusting in coworkers that tend to be 'gossip girls' and tell lies that go around the office.
EM
Social Worker
Government

Don't trust anyone to keep a secret.
SL
Assistant Manager
Food and Beverage

Don't get involved in office politics. You can't win against management and remember that managers come and go. If I like the job just hang in there and do your absolute best to be promoted.
PS
Office Administrator
Aerospace

Speak up and don't let your organization create a culture in which people are reluctant to give you bad news or unpleasant facts. It is easy to let people create a bubble around the CEO and getting out of it takes effort and focus.
ET
Senior VP
Environmental Consulting

In business, never give away private information to your customers or co-workers. As an employee you have promised secrecy of information to the business you work for.
Anonymous

Negatism®

Make the buck stop with you; share success and credit, but DON'T be afraid to stand up for yourself when you know someone is taking advantage of your 'shared credit' philosophy.
DDW
Owner
High-Tech Marketing

Don't think that standing for morals or values will increase your standing with your peers.
Anonymous
Superior Officer
Law Enforcement

Don't talk about others on a speakerphone!
Anonymous

KITCHENETTE SINK

"I have not failed.
I've just found 10,000 ways that don't work."
—*Thomas Edison*

My biggest mistake was trying early on, trying to please everyone. There are people out there, especially over the internet, who are there with good intentions and do not need your help. These people are there to see what they can steal off of you and your website. So my learning experience has been to stay helpful but stay cautious, as well.
KL
Small Business Owner
Internet Customer Service

Biggest mistake was not taking time off for me. Overworking not paying attention enough to my health. Take some time off and live.
NG
Owner
Construction Contractor

Commit. No matter what.
PW
Owner
Small Business

Avoid listening to one specific person. Ask many and think about the advice before you act.
SH
Artisan

Not setting boundaries between work and personal time. I had a job working from home, which for me translated into nonstop work, I never took time off. I felt a lot of (purely self-imposed) pressure. Other coworkers set better limits and I resented it. But the problem and the solution were both within my power. I just didn't see it at the time.
JTM
Practice Manager
Veterinary Medicine

Killed by lack of organization and follow up, which are two hugely important things in real estate.
Anonymous
Realtor

I cried at work. I feel like a child now and people treat me different when problems arise.
WW
Paralegal
Law Firm

Do not discuss business with anyone.
Anonymous

Don't trust people.
Anonymous

I must set personal boundaries with time to protect my family.
Anonymous
Private Tutor
Education

An empty time period in your resume? Don't tell the truth! Make up something uncheckable such as private lessons at your home about anything, but leave blank time such as unemployed time or job you weren't proud of or got fired from. Make up a good story lie to fill in any embarrassing blanks in time.
MJM

I wish someone had told me not to work only for a paycheck.
BC
Independent
Financial

Not following your heart or inner voice. You always know what is best, it just isn't always the conscious you.
Anonymous
Owner
Chimney Maintenance

Knowing when to get out is not the same as giving up.
TK
Owner
Retail

Lead, don't follow.
BB
Owner
Tech Sales

Stay with a business you know, or be very well trained. I tried to jump in the deep end before I could swim, and I drowned.
JP

Just because you know the business and you are good at it doesn't guarantee success; if you don't have conviction and a strong work ethic you will fail.
DJT
Owner
Restaurant

I ignored my instinct and premonitions.
RG
Owner
Construction

Not getting out soon enough and hanging on, being optimistic, and delusional.
Anonymous

I wish I always got it in writing. Now, I always follow up conversations with confirming emails stating what transpired in the phone call.
AL
Freelance
Publishing

Do ALL the homework beforehand. Researching the client after the fact is pointless.
Anonymous

Don't make commitments on behalf of a vendor. They do not have the same motivation you do.
CJ
Owner
Sales

Don't ever trust your competition to be honest / fair.
Anonymous

Pick an acronym common in your industry and ask your accountant if he knows what it means. If they do not, then you are using the wrong accountant.
Cleo
Entrepreneur
Corporate Services

Not sure what topic this belongs in, but I learn it again and again... You can't fight crazy, and you can't fight stupid. This applies to both clients and employees.
LH
Partner
Spa Resort

I would pay the extra money for auditing (we did audits every three years, reviews on the other two) and then have a systematic way to insure that the recommendations in the CPA's letter were followed.
Anonymous

If it does not make money, don't do it.
Anonymous

Don't ever take on a project (I do freelance editing/writing) without a formal contract. A handshake, even between friends, is not sufficient. There should be absolute clarity about fees, delivery time, payment time, and precise expectations for the project before you agree to take it on.
Anonymous
Publishing

Don't assume in business. Check it out. You will often find out things are not as they appear and opportunities for sales can be lost because your assumption was wrong.
RH
Owner
Pest Control

Don't start a project without a clear plan for its execution, a clear understanding of the desired outcome, and as accurate a cost analysis as possible. It is easy to get caught up in a fresh, new idea, without taking the time to analyze it properly. Even a few minutes of research can save hundreds, if not thousands, of dollars. Don't forget to ask for fresh insights from the people around you. Many of the best ideas I've implemented in the last several years weren't my ideas, but were instead the result of listening to Joe Schmoe's rambling suggestions, "It would be great if...." Don't tune out criticism or become defensive when people come to you with complaints; instead, listen carefully for the truth of such statements (even the most caustic remarks can sometimes contain something of value), ask for suggestions for improvement and don't be dismissive of the advice (however poorly delivered) you're offered for improvement.
SCS
Manager
Professional Services

Don't work the "family" out of your family. If you have a small business, family run...you have to remember whose dream it was and not assume everyone is going to be as willing as you to do the work.
AMS
Owner
Commercial Cleaning

Don't hit "reply all" when thinking it was just "reply." **Not sure this is just for business owners, but good advice anyway.**
RRR
Owner
Recording Studio

My biggest mistake? I'm quite sure I didn't make it yet!
KW
CPA
Accounting Firm

PARTNERS

"If we are together nothing is impossible.
If we are divided all will fail."
—*Winston Churchill*

Going into a business with partners who were friends. Big mistake, money changes the dynamics.
C
Owner
CrossFit Gym

Making sure the contract is filled in completely and signed.
SL
Managing Partner
Ranch

Don't go into a partnership without executed paperwork, clear expectations, and extensive vetting of your partner.
KH
Owner
Small Business

I failed to have an exit strategy. I failed to have a bookkeeping system that I could easily access financial information and make decisions based upon those facts. I learned that you have to control expenses and layoff employees when the financials say you can't afford them. I went into the business by happen-stance, I was offered a partnership and I took it without much research about the longevity of the industry in the current market.
MGB
Owner
Specialty Manufacturing

The biggest mistake I made was starting a business with close friends. Within two years the three of us were not friends anymore. I bought the other two out 15 years ago. I was able to rekindle friendship with one but haven't spoken to the second since the buyout. A lesson I learned the hard way is to never trust anyone in business. Always contemplate the angles. Nobody is your friend in business. Not all people will try to take advantage but there are many who will—nobody cares about your business but you.
JT
Owner/ Operator
Restaurant

Took someone at their word without a track record of success. Trust their word, but verify with a paper trail.
AMP

Do not go into business with a partner who does not understand that owning a cafe is an immense amount of hard work!
MH
Owning Partner
Café

Quitting at the first sign of trouble.
Anonymous

I would have a partner next time. Difficult to run a business alone.
Anonymous

Opened a winery and did not take into consideration the religion that the majority of the people in the area practiced. Had a long legal fight, which was costly. Won fight but ended up shutting the winery and destroying all the grapes.
HRD
Vintner

I did not listening to my partner who had the sense to try to talk me out of it, but I didn't listen.
DL

Doing business with the wrong people; business relationships have to be a win - win for both sides.
GB
Owner
Tool & Die Manufacturing

Biggest mistake: Going into business with a friend. The more successful we became, the greedier he got. Friendship was not really important to him anymore...Ultimately, he stole a lot more than money from me.
Anonymous
Broker
Insurance

Don't ask friends or family to help.
Anonymous

Do NOT do business with friends or family (And that includes your wife's/girlfriends' family)
JJ

I trusted the CEO of my last company who then sabotaged my practice. I should have trusted the personal opinion of my spouse, one of the few times I did not.
SMK
Owner
Healthcare

Don't hire your girl friend for anything important that requires accountability.
Anonymous

Just like marriages, having a business partner is not always easy. When times are fruitful and money is plentiful, everyone gets a long. In tough business climates and when moneys runs short - that is the real test.
Steven
Partner
Retail Chain

The biggest mistakes that I have made in start-ups is working with people who did not share the same world view and passions as I. Being an entrepreneur is an obsessive passion and when my partners and I didn't share the same passion we were not working on the same page. I have learned to be very picky in choosing work/ passion collaborators.
Cindy
Entrepreneur

I would never partner with a friend again. I would employ a friend, but never partners, again. I let my friend/partner deliver the rent payment for our space, and it wasn't being paid. She was pocketing the money. Never again.
Anonymous

I went into business with someone who was very competent at her job, like me. Neither of us wanted to do the administration or really knew how to bring in business. We have a happy ending because we were fortunate to recognize it early and hired people to do what we're not good at. If I could do it again, I would partner with someone who has different skills than me.
RR
Partner
Law Firm

I was invited into an existing partnership that was owned by two best friends. Bad idea. Any time we had a disagreement or needed to vote on something, they would stick together. It was always them versus me.
FVB
Partner
Architecture

Partners

Don't make your friend a business partner if they do not have the financial backing to support the venture. Basically, don't think you can trust someone to take care of your business the way you do. If you can do it on your own, stick with it.
AS
CFO
Retail Clothing

Don't start a small business alone — without a partner who is also invested financially and emotionally.
Linda
CEO
International Business Consulting

Don't get into a business partnership with someone! If you can't make the business survive on it's own don't do it - finding someone to count on is so very risky.
BR
Owner/ Pastry Chef
Artisan Bakery

I wish I had never partnered.
Anonymous

Don't go into business with your friends.
Anonymous

ABOUT THE AUTHOR

Kevin owns a CPA firm in Trumbull, CT. There he services small businesses, with a specialty in advertising, marketing, design, programming, online retail and other creative industries. Kevin Wenig CPA LLC is consistently rated in the Top 20 Accounting Firms in Fairfield County by the Fairfield County Business Journal.

He also owns Finance Office Partners, which provides a complete outsourced finance department for small and mid-sized businesses. A complete Finance Department just like the big guys have... but for small guys.

Founder and CEO of CPApp, LLC - a software company that creates online applications for the accounting industry.

Created the first iPhone app for taxes called "Tax Vault." Take a picture of your business receipt and it gets e-mailed to your CPA. *Spend it and Send It!* Also gets the distinction of being CPApp's first project that actually generated revenue!

Founded National Bean Counter's Day – April 16th. A day to celebrate your favorite accountant. (And it seemed like a good idea at the time!)

Advisor to Intuit as part of their Professional Advisor Program.

Also hired by Intuit to create and run webinars to teach other accountants how to bring technology into their own practices.

Founded Negatism. The hobby project that took on a life of its own. For better or for worse.

Kevin lives in Easton, CT with his wife and two children. There he splits his time being a CPA, thinking of new ideas to distract himself and looking for his golf ball.